CREATED

FOR

MISSION

Effective Models for Districts and Leaders

GUSTAVO CROCKER
BOB BROADBOOKS

BEACON HILL PRESS
OF KANSAS CITY

Cover Design: Kevin Williamson
Interior Design: Sharon Page

Library of Congress Cataloging-in-Publication Data

Crocker, Gustavo, 1963-
    Created for mission : effective models for districts and leaders / Gustavo Crocker, Bob Broadbooks.
        p. cm.
    Includes bibliographical references (p.   ).
    ISBN 978-0-8341-2824-8 (pbk.)
    1. Church of the Nazarene—Government. I. Broadbooks, Bob. II. Title.
    BX8699.N35B76 2011
    262'.0799—dc23
                                                    2011034127

10 9 8 7 6 5 4 3 2 1

Contents

Foreword

Gustavo Crocker and Bob Broadbooks have written a book whose time has come! In a day when denominations are searching for identity, they have penned a definitive masterpiece on the purpose and mission of a district in the context of the global church.

This is a book for every district superintendent and district advisory board member who wants to lead effectively. I love the three-six-six emphasis because it encourages every district to step out from the crowd of look-alikes and become all that Christ would have them to be.

Every reader should pay special attention to the "Six Marks of a Healthy District" and use these insights as a guide for reviewing the current operation of their district. Also, the "Six Essential Characteristics of a District Superintendent" will provide plenty of discussion materials for those who want to measure their effectiveness as district leaders and consider growth possibilities.

"Why Districts?" will challenge the assumptions and operational mode of every denominational leader who wants to move from the status quo to a missional focused organization. This book is a sterling reminder that the time has come for districts to become missional focused instead of being buried in administrative detail.

Finally, as I read the book, I was inspired to believe that those who read its pages will rediscover the biblical and missiological purpose of a district. I encourage you to read it with an open mind and ask God to give you the insight to grow your district and to become a model of missional effectiveness for others to follow.

Dr. Stan Toler
General Superintendent
Church of the Nazarene

Preface

Gustavo Crocker and Bob Broadbooks have written a challenging missional book that explores the purpose and function of districts within the Church of the Nazarene. The clustering of congregations into districts has been a denominational practice for over a century. From time to time, however, some pastors and lay leaders have questioned the value of the district and the role of the district superintendent. Have there been times when the cost of a district was greater than the missional value added to the life of local churches?

This timely book is an attempt to help the global church rediscover the biblical and missiological purposes of the *district as an agent of mission*. The driving concern is to transform the district from being a purely administrative entity to an effective missional agency.

The district's role and function in areas where amazing growth movements are taking place is quite different from the maintenance mentality that often sets in after several generations. Gustavo and Bob are giving us excellent tools to attempt to reverse that process and return to the original apostolic function of the district primarily as a missional agency.

They address three compelling reasons for districts while exploring and "unpacking" a visionary definition of *district*. Then, the authors study and build on the results of an evaluation of several vigorously growing districts in order to provide a good foundation for leaders and their districts to grow into missional effectiveness for the sake of God's mission. This study results in identifying health indicators of "Districts as MODELS."

Because institutional success is heavily connected to leadership, the authors also focus on some essential characteristics of an effective district superintendent. As in earlier chapters, this theoretical framework is enriched with fascinating anecdotal narratives that bring the teaching to life while exploring six qualities of fruitful missional superintendents.

Finally, the appendix includes a very useful "District Development Self-Study Survey." This tool has been field-tested in many districts around the world, and it will provide us with a preliminary district missional health checkup.

We often tend to focus on districts as agents of governance. The *Manual of the Church of the Nazarene* would certainly affirm that important but secondary role. The tragedy is when districts become primarily governance agencies that protect and maintain the status quo. This book will help us rediscover the primary and imperative missional role of a district. I celebrate this candid and insightful perspective that will help us evaluate our districts and also give us all practical tools to strengthen and transform our districts into apostolic agents of our Lord's mission, to the glory of God!

Jerry D. Porter
General Superintendent
Church of the Nazarene

Introduction

Since its establishment in 1908, the Church of the Nazarene has been organized into districts, partially for geographical reasons, but primarily because of the ecclesiological background of those who joined the denomination at its point of creation. According to Nazarene historical records, the newly merged denomination was established with 10,034 members, organized in 228 congregations, and clustered in eleven districts. Consequently, for many Nazarenes, being part of a district is synonymous with being a Nazarene.

As the denomination grew (geographically and in age), it became apparent that it was necessary to review, restate, and reaffirm the role that districts previously played, currently play, and will continue to play in the strategy and mission of the Church of the Nazarene worldwide. Several projects and documents have helped leaders understand and promote the importance of the district in the life of our denomination. Some of them have been administrative in nature, while others have provided theological and biblical basis for superintendency.

This book, however, is an attempt to help district leadership rediscover the biblical and missiological purposes of the district *as an agent of mission*. Our desire is to build upon these prior works and help the current generation of Nazarenes around the world embrace districts as models of missional effectiveness. We want to do so by introducing not only the value of a district from a missiological and biblical perspective but also the importance of moving forward with missional effectiveness and excellence.

We realized that in order to move from being a purely administrative entity to an effective missional agency, districts and their leaders may have to take an intentional leap (beyond the norm) in their thinking, their scope, and their activities. To help them, this book explores "Three Reasons for Districts," "Six Marks of a Healthy District," and "Six Essential Characteristics of an Effective District Superintendent." It is our hope that when districts and their leaders review the following materials, they and their districts will become effective agents of mission and transformation in the name of Christ.

Gustavo Crocker
Bob Broadbooks

THREE REASONS
FOR DISTRICTS

1 ❧ Districts: Their Purpose

"Our church is a denomination of local churches organized into districts." We have heard this statement many times at district assemblies, district gatherings, and even at the dinner table when trying to explain to others the concept of the district. While the idea of a district may sound familiar to many who have been a part of the Church of the Nazarene for some time, the idea of a district sounds foreign to believers in pioneer missionary works or even unnecessary for those who are part of large, self-contained, growing congregations in the West.

Like most institutions that survived the twentieth century, the district has not escaped being scrutinized by some who don't see the value of investing in yet another layer of church bureaucracy. Yet, there are more reasons than pragmatic, business ones that factor into the necessity of districts. We need to explore a broader view of districts than the purely financial or institutional bottom line.

Districts ensure that the current and future generations of church members can continually maximize God's resources for the sake of our mission to "make Christlike disciples in the nations."[1]

2 ⇜ *Why Districts?*

Throughout its history, the church has created structures and strategies to fulfill the Great Commission to "go into all the world and preach the good news to all creation" (Mark 16:15). From the sending model that Jesus used with the Twelve and the seventy to the geographical delegation models employed by Paul in his missionary endeavors, these strategies have not been designed to create ecclesiological hierarchies but to facilitate the mission of the church. A survey of the letter to Titus, for example, suggests that geographical jurisdictions (judicatories or districts) were designed to enable the church to grow in both breadth and depth according to Christ's commission and within the orthodoxy of a sound doctrine. Districts are more than structures or bureaucratic layers. Districts are agencies of the church created for mission strategy, synergy, and unity.

REASONS DISTRICTS ARE CREATED

1. For Missional Strategy

Titus was a Christian worker who had traveled with Paul during his missionary journeys. Both Paul and Titus began the work in Crete, and when it was time for Paul to continue his journey, the work needed continuity and development. As a good missionary, Paul established a new judicatory in Crete and left Titus responsible for its continued development. This appointment was later formalized in the early church as that of a bishop or an overseer.

Paul's instructions to Titus were clear: "The reason I left you in Crete was that you might straighten out what was left unfinished and appoint elders in every town, as I directed you" (Titus 1:5). In other words, the reason for appointing an overseer was primarily missional. Titus's job was to provide organization and oversight to the missionary work in the land by ensuring that the new believers were nurtured and discipled, the local expressions of the church were strengthened, and appropriate leadership was appointed. Titus's job was to ensure that all of this would happen, as directed by Paul.

This verse captures the essence of districts and judicatories as entities of mission: (*a*) they must be developmental, (*b*) they must be structured, and (*c*) they must be accountable.

- First, developmentally, districts are not finished products, and even the mission is not an end to itself. The redemptive work of God on this earth continues through the church, and districts help the various organic expressions of the body of Christ continue the work that was begun through missional engagement. Missional work is messy. It has ups and downs. It shows quick initial results but messy conflicts in the process. It is never finished. The main reason for establishing missional structures is to develop, strengthen, and help bring order to the chaos resulting from the work that has been started.
- Second, systems and structures are important accessories to sound mission strategy. While the role of the district is to help congregations fulfill God's transforming mission in their communities, the sustainability of the work is maximized through effective organizational systems. "Appointing elders in every town" could be interpreted as the cultural equivalent of "organized delegation."
  - In the Old Testament, cities were ruled and judged by their elders, those with the greatest wisdom and experience in the commu-

nity. By the New Testament period, prominent older men in the synagogues were called "elders." Paul followed the convenient, conventional forms of synagogue leadership in his culture rather than instituting entirely foreign leadership structures. "In every city" meant that the different house churches in each city would each have their own leaders.[1]

- Third, the missional dimension of a district requires accountability to the broader body of believers. Just as Paul, Barnabas, and other missionaries of the church were accountable to the church in Jerusalem (and also to the church in Antioch, which had sent them), Paul delegated a missionary function to Titus. Terms like *interdependence* and *connectedness* are implicit in Paul's instructions to Titus. Titus was to run the work in Crete not as an independent missionary but as a delegated overseer on behalf of the universal church. "As I directed you" implies accountability, delegation, and submission.

A Story

The Church of the Nazarene in Guatemala was established in 1904 when missionaries Richard and Ann Anderson arrived in the country. Six years later and with only a few converts, the Church of the Nazarene was able to purchase a small piece of land in the remote central plains of the country. It was not until August 10, 1919 (fifteen years later), that missionary John Franklin organized the first Church of the Nazarene in Guatemala. While it took years to organize the first congregation, at the time of their centennial celebration in 2004, more than sixty-five thousand Nazarenes worshipped in the country.[2]

The strategy behind this sustained and deep growth had two basic components: (*a*) leadership development and (*b*) district development. First of all, the missionary strategy of the Church of the Nazarene has historically relied on training and enabling local leaders. While missionaries have gone and sacrificially invested their lives in sharing Christ with people in pioneer areas, they have intentionally worked at identifying, training, empowering, and enabling local leaders to carry on God's mission through the church. Missionaries have always known that "the best seed comes from the harvest itself."[3] As a result, a field that took over a decade to embrace the gospel now has hundreds of national leaders who are impacting their church locally and globally.

Second, the mission strategy of the denomination has focused on developing districts as strategic entities. As part of this intentional focus, and following the biblical model of Titus 1, the Guatemala District became the first Nazarene mission field to have a national district superintendent, Rev. Federico Guillermo, appointed in 1960.[4] This process continued when, under the leadership of Dr. Jerald Johnson in the 1970s, the Nazarene denomination adopted a four-step process for districts to attain regular status.[5] Again, the Guatemala District was the first to reach such a milestone, and, in 1974, the Guatemala District was officially declared the first regular district in a World Mission area.

The intentional focus on leadership and district development has taken the missionary work in Guatemala from one district and less than five thousand members in 1974 to eleven districts and seventy-seven thousand members in 2010. It took pioneer missionaries seventy years to grow from five to five thousand members. When the district reached its maturity in 1974 and began multiplying, it took them thirty years to sponsor the creation of ten more districts (an average of one new district every three years) and to add seventy-two thousand new members (an average of twenty-four hundred new members every year).

2. For Synergy

One of the common questions that pastors and leaders in older fields ask is, "What is the value of a district?" For many of them, their churches have grown to a point that no longer requires the missional impetus and organization that a district provides. This argument is understandable, but only for those congregations that have reached such a level of health and development that they can perform most of the functions that the district would provide for an average congregation. But what happens when such a strong and financially viable church faces a crisis? What happens when the leader of the church moves on? History teaches us that current organizational health is not necessarily a sign of longevity. For example, when Paul wrote to the Ephesians, they were a great model of congregational vibrancy and mission, but John's Revelation describes the church in Ephesus as a church that has forgotten its first love (see Rev. 2:4).

At the same time, scores of small congregations cannot survive on their own as they attempt to minister both locally and globally. A synergistic entity such as a judicatory or district enables small or weak churches to join forces to maximize God's redeeming work in their communities and beyond.

This synergistic value is important to both small and large churches alike.

Synergy is a biblical concept (*synergy* from the Greek word *sunergos*—"to work with"). In fact, Paul used it often to describe the collaborative nature of the mission to the Gentiles. In 1 Corinthians 3:9, Paul reminds the church that we are God's "fellow workers." In Philippians 2:25-30, he uses the same term to refer to Epaphroditus as a symbol of collaboration and partnership in mission. In other words, God's redemptive mission requires the collaborative participation of the body of believers as we partner with him in sharing the good news.

Ecclesiastes 4:9-12 provides a vivid picture of the value of synergy: "Two are better than one, because they have a good return for their work: If one falls down, his friend can help him up. But pity the man who falls and has no one to help him up! Also, if two lie down together, they will keep warm. But how can one keep warm alone? Though one may be overpowered, two can defend themselves. A cord of three strands is not quickly broken."

The synergistic work of mission results in lighter loads, maximized resources, and mobilized congregations.

- Synergy distributes the missional load. One person or one church alone cannot effectively share the good news to all humanity.

- Synergy maximizes limited missional resources. If all individuals and churches put their resources together, their results will be immeasurably larger than the results of even the largest and strongest single congregation in a given location.
- Synergy mobilizes a larger number of missional resources. Motivation is contagious. Exciting stories of those who engage in missional activity motivate others—even those who never saw themselves getting involved—to become active participants in God's mission.

A Story

At the heart of the history of the Church of the Nazarene, the Los Angeles District has modeled the value of collaboration and synergy. Their story of a district-wide work team, as told by one of the team leaders, says it well:

We celebrate partnerships between the Church of the Nazarene and other organizations. Having planned and participated in a local church *JESUS* film trip, I was very much aware of the impact this partnership has on the world. The district had the ability to partner and raise funds to send multiple teams. Our goal was to send a district adult team and a district youth team.

We were able to raise enough funds to send five sets of *JESUS* film equipment.

One main advantage was an opportunity to unite the district. We encouraged a member from each of our language groups to attend, and encouraged all churches within that language group to join together and raise funds to support that team member. We created a diverse, fun team and an opportunity to share cultures within our district, while sharing the love of Christ with Sri Lanka.

A district team provides more resources. There are so many who cannot go that can send, and so many individual churches that cannot raise the funds and send a team, but that can support a project and send a team member. We were able to represent the Los Angeles District, a unified district that supports the work of Christ.[6]

3. To Foster Unity and Doctrinal Accountability

One of the immediate results of effective missional work is chaos. In fact, congregations with a sense of mission are always on the cutting edge. When there is movement, there is friction, noise, tension, and risk. The problem is that most of us are not comfortable with the chaos that comes with effective mission. We wish for good results and great stories, but we would love to be spared the mess resulting from radical change, radical obedience, and radical witnessing.

Paul, the missionary, instructed Titus, the overseer of the church in Crete, to "straighten out what was left unfinished" (Titus 1:5, NIV) or "half-done" (TM). It is obvious that Paul's work had been effective in planting the seed to start a holy revolt and revival in the cities in Crete, but he had to move on. Consequently, further organization was needed.

Titus's primary job was to facilitate the work of the church in all cities by appointing elders who met clearly-stated criteria, by developing appropriate norms of conduct, by teaching sound doctrine, and by displaying godly character (all within the context of the people of Crete). This facilitating role would in turn result in "those who have trusted in God may be careful to devote themselves to doing what is good" (3:8). Thus, a district that fosters unity and orthodoxy:

- Emphasizes character and doctrinal orthodoxy in the appointment of elders (1:5-9).
- Ensures that godly, scriptural lifestyles are promoted through the development of contextual codes of conduct and appropriate discipline (vv. 10-14).
- Teaches sound doctrine (2:1).

- Disciples people of all ages and walks of life: older men (v. 2), older women (v. 4), younger women (v. 4), younger men (v. 6), those who are employed (v. 9), and those under authority (3:1).
- Encourages and rebukes with scriptural authority (2:15).
- Avoids foolish controversies about the Law (3:9).
- Promotes godliness among all believers, in order that they may live productive lives (v. 14).

A Story

The Mid-Atlantic in the US/Canada Region is an example of missional intention. Their mission statement focuses on intentionality and challenges churches in the district to join the movement of God in that part of the country. Their missional activities foster those principles in pastors, leaders, and those preparing for ministry. The direct result is higher-than-average numbers of leaders called to full-time ministry; churches and individuals engaged in church planting, evangelism, and discipleship; and leaders willing to embrace new missional paradigms that respond to the needs of the communities they serve.

Since his arrival in the Mid-Atlantic District (formerly the Washington District) in 1997, Ken

Mills has focused on intentional mission engagement. This intentionality is reflected in the district's Mission and Vision Statements:

The purpose of the Mid-Atlantic District Church of the Nazarene is to advance the ministry of Jesus Christ through local churches.

Core values:

- Intentional proclamation of scriptural holiness
- Intentional engagement in mission
- Intentional encouragement and development of pastors and leaders
- Intentional provision for team ministry
- Intentional emphasis on communication
- Intentional focus on accountability

Compelled by God we seek to be a movement of God's people who passionately live in the story of Jesus Christ. The vision for impacting the Mid-Atlantic region includes:

- **Rethinking** mental models to facilitate versatile and adaptable congregations that give new opportunities for God's movement . . .
- **Reproducing and multiplying** pastors, leaders, churches, and disciples . . . equipping, empowering, and sending them to the harvest . . .

- **Partnering and collaborating** with each other, with other churches, and groups outside the local congregation to actualize the movement that God is already creating in this Mid-Atlantic region . . . ***Moving with God now!***[7]

We have seen how this focus brings churches together for missional engagement, encourages believers to respond to the call for service, and moves communities toward transformation. In a country where many districts are closing churches and experiencing declines in membership, the Mid-Atlantic District has been able to rally the congregations together around mission, sound doctrine, and collaboration.

3 ⇌ *What Is a District?*

In order for local congregations to operate beyond their closed circle of influence and accomplish God's mission of redemption and transformation, they must come together, maximize God's resources, and foster unity in the midst of diversity. The concept of a geographic judicatory (or district) helps achieve those purposes. Using the previous biblical and organizational exploration as a background, the Church of the Nazarene defines a district as follows: "A district is an entity made up of interdependent local churches organized to facilitate the mission of each local church through mutual support, the sharing of resources, and collaboration."[1]

This definition includes several key terms that are worth considering separately:

1. **An entity.** Districts exemplify the metaphor of a gathering. They are flexible and dynamic. When people talk about the district, they should be talking about the gathering, the ag-

gregate of all the churches and congregations that form it. We know that as the church has gotten older and the concept of the district has become part of the members' common language, some people think of it as either the district superintendent or the district office, but the reality is that the district is neither. When the churches assemble, celebrate together, and synergize, they are the district.

2. **Made up of interdependent local churches.** The beauty of a district is that it fosters interdependency. Without such an agency, churches would fall into the two dangerous extremes that tend to weaken the church: dependence and independence. The problem of dependence is that congregations do not move beyond the paternalistic constraints of the parent organization, while the problem of complete independence is that independent churches lack doctrinal, organizational, and financial accountability. Interdependence, on the other hand, allows each individual congregation to contextually respond to the realities of its community while remaining connected to a network of support, accountability, and biblical orthodoxy.

3. **Organized to facilitate the mission of each local church.** Districts are not ends to them-

selves. The reason churches gather in districts is so that the sum of all parts can assist each individual congregation in accomplishing its mission. There is no district mission without aggregate congregational missions. There are no conversions or baptisms at the district office. The actual missional activity happens at the heart of every local congregation, and the role of the district is to ensure that each congregation fulfills its transforming mission in the community.

4. **Through mutual support, the sharing of resources, and collaboration.** One of the great contributions of denominationalism is the opportunity for local congregations to benefit from the exchange of best practices and resources for the purpose of accomplishing God's mission in their communities. Churches come together in the agency of a district to gather their resources and experience, so that the local and global mission can be accomplished as the sum of all parts.

When districts fulfill these functions, the question of the added value of the district is minimized, and the district moves from an institution to a missional agency. However, realizing their purpose is just the first step for districts to become true agents of mission facilitation. Effective districts are those that not only understand their purpose but also move to fulfill it in healthy and effective ways. The following section introduces us to the marks of a healthy district.

SIX MARKS OF A HEALTHY DISTRICT

4 ⮞ Districts as MODELS:
The Marks of a Healthy District

Organizations become what they measure. If institutions focus on numbers and growth, they will naturally experience numeric growth. If their focus is on health, they will tend to show it as defined and measured. For example, the *Manual of the Church of the Nazarene* provides clear, quantitative guidelines for recognizing the various phases in the life of a district. While Nazarenes have historically focused on these quantitative standards of district maturity, many of us overlook the fact that the *Manual* also establishes qualitative parameters to determine the health and maturity of a district. A recent addition to the *Manual* states that, "Leadership, infrastructure, budgetary responsibility, and doctrinal integrity must be demonstrated"[1] in order for a district to attain maturity status.

Because of this oversight, the practice of district development around the world has primarily focused on districts reaching the numeric benchmarks to be considered mature and self-supported. One of the reasons for this common practice is that while the numeric requirements are clear, the qualitative indicators for mature districts are not defined around specific parameters to meet such criteria.

In studying church development around the world, and particularly in Europe and North America, it became apparent that there are numerous frameworks for church health and development. Most of these frameworks even include their own assessment tools that local churches and groups can apply to determine their health and viability. However, very little has been written with regard to organizational health of districts as agencies of mission and synergy.

Motivated by the need to reinject missional effectiveness and encouraged by the implicit qualitative requirements stated in the *Manual of the Church of the Nazarene*, leaders of the church in the Eurasia and US/Canada regions have worked together to test and identify those key health indicators that districts must evidence, regardless of their phase. The list, while not exhaustive, provides a good foundation for leaders and their districts to review, assess, and grow into missional effectiveness for the sake of God's mission. The indicators of districts as MODELS are:

Missional Definition

Organizational Effectiveness

Doctrinal Integrity

Educational Priority

Leadership Excellence, and

Spiritual Vibrancy

MISSIONAL DEFINITION

Mission is at the heart of what we do. God's mission throughout the entire biblical story and the long history of humanity is to restore his creation. God is a God with a mission. As part of his mission for our time and our generation, God has entrusted the church to be the bearer of the good news of his accomplished mission—the incarnate Jesus who died and rose again to restore us to a perfect relation with the Father. God is a missionary God; Jesus came with a clear redemptive mission; the Holy Spirit empowers us to fulfill his mission. This sense of mission and purpose must also be part of the life of the church!

In a healthy district, churches must be able to reflect and articulate a clear sense of mission and purpose. This sense of mission is greatly influenced by congregations embracing God's mission, the denominational mission, the mission and strategic priorities of the district, and of course, their own local mission. A district without a sense of mission is only a bureaucratic structure.

But mission alone is not enough. Model districts are also able to envision their future in such a way that local congregations transform the vision into specific ministry goals, because mission alone does not result in change.[2] It is imperative for district leaders to help churches develop and own a sense of corporate vision for the future:

By "vision" we mean a shared picture of the future you seek to create—what you believe [the district] can accomplish. As people within your [district] create a clear and compelling picture of the [district and congregation's] future, they become committed to helping that future occur.

A clear sense of mission and purpose also guides [pastors and their congregations] in making everyday choices about which [ministry] opportunities they will pursue.[3]

We had the opportunity to meet with an outstanding district superintendent whose passion for inspiring and challenging his district for missional engagement was evident by the way the mission statement was persistently presented at every event, in every report, and in every piece of district correspondence. There was something missing, however. The mission statement was clear and inspirational, but it still begged the "so what?" question. When challenged to start painting the future picture of the district, the district superintendent assembled a vision-casting team that helped him dream the dream and paint it in such a way that congregations and their members could also dream it, see it, and embrace it.

How is missional definition evident in a model district? A district with a sense of mission encourages its congregations to become actively concerned with evangelism, discipleship, church planting, leadership development, and the development of healthy congregations. In other words, a district with a missional intention helps congregations move from a "maintenance model to a faithfulness/fruitfulness model"[4] by doing the following:

- Changing the paradigm of current expectations. In the past, district leaders and their staff have been measured in terms of meetings and visits they had with pastors and congregations. In fact, there have been district assemblies where the district superintendent and the district leadership spend most of their time reporting on the number of visits and board meetings held during the year. Under the a new paradigm, district leaders and their teams would be measured in terms of effective facilitation of missional engagement on behalf of the congregations under their oversight.

- Taking responsibility for results. Dr. Jerry Porter, general superintendent for the Church of the Nazarene, writes: "Leaders must confront obstacles and take responsibility for results. It is easier to fulfill a customary role, even if we are not seeing the results God desires. However, when we move from our comfort zones to obedience zones we feel fearful, and Satan tells us to get 'back in the box . . .' We are tempted to place on God the full responsibility for results. God gives the increase, but we must plant and water the seedlings."[5]

- Shifting from administrative direction to the facilitation of church development. Perhaps the biggest paradigm shift in helping districts engage missionally is for leaders to move from being efficient administrators to effective congregational consultants who will facilitate transformation and mission for the churches in the district.

- Sharing the vision with consistency and persistency. Having a vision and a passion for a missional church is not enough. To get the average pastor and church member to capture the vision requires consistency, persistency, and feedback. In reality, not everyone catches the vision at the first glimpse. We have learned that most people embrace the vision in stages:

○ The first time they see it, the vision is a **snap-shot**

○ The second time, the vision becomes an **idea**

○ The third time, the vision becomes a **picture**

○ The fourth time, the vision becomes a **design**

○ The fifth time, the vision becomes a **blueprint**

○ The sixth time, the vision becomes a **project**

○ The seventh time, the vision becomes a **reality**[6]

In evaluating its missional clarity and effectiveness, districts and their leaders must ask themselves the following questions:[7]

• What is the spoken and unspoken (written and unwritten) mission of the district in fifteen words or less? How is it communicated? How often?

• Can we trace the direct influence of the district mission to local church missional activities? Give examples or stories.

• Do churches in the district recognize their missional role as inspired by the mission statement? How do you know?

• To what degree is there a clear and compelling vision at work that inspires passion and gives direction to our congregations?

• Do churches in the district have specific evangelism, church planting, discipleship, and community engagement plans that are reflective of their missional commitment?

ORGANIZATIONAL EFFECTIVENESS

Architecture students are exposed early on to the design mantra, "form follows function."[8] The same is true for organizations. In a healthy, mature district, organization follows mission. This means that the organizational arrangements of a model district must reflect mission intentionality, administrative consistency, and a contextual understanding of the local organizational and legal realities in which the Church of the Nazarene operates.

In their landmark piece on organizational excellence, Peters and Waterman suggest that entities move beyond mediocrity when they set their basic mission and when they create the organizational arrangements capable of facilitating and fulfilling such mission.[9] A recent study conducted among successful Christian ministries in the early 2000s proves that the axiom is also true for districts and local ministries. The study found that effective Christian organizations that thrive beyond mere survival display structures and organizational arrangements that focus on the mission and purpose of the ministry and not on maintaining the organization itself.[10] In these ministries, roles, boards, teams, and flows of services were found to be more important than titles and hierarchies. On the other hand, failing and mediocre organizations that were part of the study displayed organizational arrangements that were primarily designed to maintain the status quo, engage in day-to-day management and preservation, and focus on individual titles and positions instead of the mission of the organization. In other words, the structure and administration of failing ministries were more nominal than functional.

The connection between form and mission in model districts can be seen in the way districts organize their various mission delivery systems to help churches accomplish their missional task. For example, while maintenance districts have the same structures and boards that model districts have as prescribed by denominational manuals and other policies and procedures, these boards and structures act significantly as mission-blockers and tradition-keepers that focus more on the board or committee itself than on the mission. In model districts, boards, entities, and even new organizational forms are designed with the sole purpose of facilitating mission at the local, district, and global levels.

Model districts also promote full life stewardship from the moment they are organized. Full life stewardship includes an intentional focus on reaching congregational self-support, district self-support, and connected giving to the various denominational causes. Healthy districts connect their financial priorities with their missional priority. In other words, model districts put their money where their mouth is. A ministry colleague used to say: "Show me the balance sheet in your checkbook and I will tell you where your missional priorities are." What this means is that a district can use the missional language and preach missional engagement but, at the end of the day, if the majority of the district resources are used to support administration and maintenance as opposed to mission, the missional language is just that: missional rhetoric.

Healthy districts are known for intentionally developing ongoing mechanisms to ensure administrative and financial integrity and accountability. Because districts have historically evolved from missional organisms to administrative entities, it is not easy to distinguish the role that such administrative systems play in defining excellent model districts. However, a closer look at those districts that balance mission and administration helps us differentiate them: for most effective, missional districts, administrative systems focus on facilitating strategic planning, financial planning, financial integrity, accountability, and evaluation. Conversely, struggling entities use administrative systems for compliance, basic auditing, and day-to-day management.

One such example of administrative effectiveness in districts is the way in which personnel and properties are managed. An informal survey of district superintendents in North America revealed that the vast majority of the district superintendent's time is spent in personnel placement (finding pastors for the various congregations), property matters, and legal issues. What worsens matters is that these issues resurface time and time again, and the district superintendents spend most of their productive time as operational managers (at best) or as white-water managers (crisis managers) at worst.

While the answer to the question of too much administrative minutia varies from location to location and from culture to culture, several common practices are worth mentioning:

- District superintendents must focus on the big picture. They must lead processes that will result in proper personnel systems, property systems, and legal systems, but a team needs to be in place to help manage the implementation of these systems. In some locations, administrative staff will be responsible for the implementation of the systems. In others, district teams should be empowered to work with the district superintendent in implementing the systems. An administrative team (or support system) releases the superintendent to focus on mission and vision casting.

- Districts must document their procedures, processes, and training systems. Most administrative issues are recurrent, and leaders spend large amounts of time reinventing the wheel. Proper documentation of processes, cases, personnel matters, and training systems help members of the district team, churches, and leaders provide continuity, efficiency, and information.

- Districts must balance strategy and operations. The main purpose of effective administrative systems is to assist with ongoing mission strategy and development. However, highlighting the strategic nature of administration needs to be done without abdicating the district's commitment to accountability and integrity.

In evaluating their organizational effectiveness, districts and their leaders are encouraged to ask themselves the following questions:

- How is the district organized for mission implementation?

- To what degree do district boards, committees, and organizations reflect the mission priority of the district? How do you measure their missional effectiveness and integration?

- What are the mechanisms that the district uses to receive feedback on the fulfillment of its missional priorities? Are there other teams or groups that help the district accomplish and review its missional priorities (e.g., mission strategy, re-visioning board, etc.)?

- What are the platforms that the district uses to allow new missional ideas to take place within the ministry of the church in the district?

- What activities of the district superintendent and staff are on target missionally? What activities of the district superintendent and staff tend to move them off mission?

- Is the district budget reflective of the missional priorities of the district? What portion of your funds should be spent directly on missional activities? What percentage is actually spent for this purpose rather than overhead?

DOCTRINAL INTEGRITY

A contemporary misconception is thinking that "all we need is to become missional." While it is true that the Church of the Nazarene needs to reignite its missional passion and vision for a transformed world, we cannot do so at the expense of the doctrine—the core belief system that has helped the Church of the Nazarene remain faithful and connected through the centuries and through social, political, and economic changes. In other words, as it was explained before, because missional work is messy and chaotic, it must be accompanied by a clear support and articulation of the doctrine of the denomination. A. W. Tozer puts it clearly in his statement about the importance of sound doctrine:

The word doctrine means simply religious beliefs held and taught. It is the sacred task of all Christians, first as believers and then as teachers of religious beliefs, to be certain that these beliefs correspond exactly to truth. A precise agreement between belief and fact constitutes soundness in doctrine. We cannot afford to have less . . .

Little by little evangelical Christians these days are being brainwashed. One evidence is that increasing numbers of them are becoming ashamed to be found unequivocally on the side of truth. They say they believe but their beliefs have been so diluted as to be impossible of clear definition.

Moral power has always accompanied definitive beliefs. Great saints have always been dogmatic. We need right now a return to a gentle dogmatism that smiles while it stands stubborn and firm on the Word of God that liveth and abideth forever.[11]

As stated in earlier chapters, teaching and promoting sound doctrine is one of the most important roles of a district. Thus, in a model district, the average congregation promotes the doctrine and core values of the Church of the Nazarene not as an imposition, but as a conscious demonstration of the congregation's belonging to and believing in those core principles that bind them together. They do so because the entity responsible for connectedness, unity, and orthodoxy (in this case the district) has fulfilled its facilitating, teaching, inspiring, and even enforcing role.

In practical terms, model districts encourage congregations to promote and study the denomination's Articles of Faith, Core Values, and the essential doctrine. Districts also foster the proper environments for theological dialogue; whereby, pastors, leaders, and congregants are able to discover, engage, and embrace the central beliefs of the church universal, as well as those of the denomination they join and serve.

Some of the questions that districts and their leaders need to ask when assessing their doctrinal consistency are:

- What methods, practices, and means does the district employ to maintain and promote doctrinal integrity before the churches?

- What is the strategy that the district employs to articulate and promote the core beliefs and values (Christian, holiness, missional) of the Church of the Nazarene?
- To what degree are lay leaders in our congregations familiar with and committed to the agreed Statement of Belief? Articles of Faith? Core Values?
- What are some ways the district superintendent engages pastors in theological reflection and development of a pastoral theology consistent with our Nazarene identity?
- How does the district ensure that new church plants are grounded in the core doctrine of the Church of the Nazarene?

EDUCATIONAL PRIORITY

While serving in global missions, Dr. Donald Owens, general superintendent emeritus of the Church of the Nazarene, often shared the view that "the sustainability of our missionary work is not measured only by the number of new churches that we plant and establish but also (and primarily) by the number of local ministers that we train and ordain." This statement reflects the historical commitment of the Church of Christ to equip, train, and encourage those called to serve as ambassadors of God's grace. In fact, an anecdotal review of modern Christianity reveals the direct correlation between the longevity of denominations and their ability to recruit, train, and ordain those called to serve as ministers of the gospel under their doctrinal coverage. The dramatic drop of members called and preparing for ministry is one of the most palpable evidences of a drop in membership and denominational vitality.

The mission of the Church of the Nazarene is to make Christlike disciples in the nations. To fulfill this mission, churches must emphasize the importance of discipleship and ministerial preparation. The *Manual of the Church of the Nazarene* highlights such importance: "The perpetuity and efficiency of the Church of the Nazarene depend largely upon the spiritual qualifications, the character, and the manner of life of its ministers."[12]

Furthermore: "Ministerial education is designed to assist in the preparation of God-called ministers whose service is vital to the expansion and extension of the holiness message into new areas of evangelistic opportunity . . . Much of the preparation is primarily theological and biblical in character, leading toward ordination in the ministry of the Church of the Nazarene."[13]

In practical terms, model districts foster intentional programs that help new believers grow from infants in the faith to ministers of the gospel. In that regard, healthy districts exhibit intentionality in discipleship, lay training, and especially ministerial preparation on a continuous basis. When reviewing their educational priority, districts and their leaders should dialogue around the following questions:

- What is the district's strategy to recruit, mentor, and train leaders for ministry service? Include comments about education toward ordination, curriculum, reading materials, and district-sponsored workshops or seminars.

- What mechanisms does the district have to help its pastors understand, share, and adequately articulate the central doctrines of the Church of the Nazarene?

- What is the district strategy for providing continuing education and training for ministers?

- How do you describe the relationship of the district to its theological education institutions?

- What are the tracks available for preparation for ordination? Do they include the major language groups of the district?

- Are there specific educational initiatives in the district designed to prepare ministers and laypersons for evangelism, church planting, and community outreach?

LEADERSHIP EXCELLENCE

Today we face the sad reality that excellent servant leadership is in short supply. Unfortunately, this is neither new nor unique of specific sectors in the secular world. God has always called servant leaders who would lead his people (1 Sam. 13:14; Ezek. 22:30; and Judg. 6:14, to name a few). The reality is that as much as mission, vision, education, systems, and doctrine are inherent qualities of a model district, their facilitation, execution, and follow-up rest on the shoulders of leadership—the district superintendents, the local pastors, and their leadership teams; or as Borden puts it: "Leadership, leadership, leadership."[14]

Leadership is crucial in developing model districts, but not just any kind of leadership. The next chapter will cover in detail the essential characteristics of those called to lead districts as missional entities. In the meantime, it is important to highlight that leadership excellence is not an exclusive requirement of district superintendents. It is an imperative for district teams, local church leadership, and pastors who, in turn, pass it on to the church members with the hope and intention to develop them into excellent servant leaders. The excellent servant leaders who our districts and churches need are:

- Leaders who lead with mission

- Leaders who lead strategically
- Leaders who lead by example
- Leaders who develop other leaders
- Leaders who turn small and unhealthy congregations into vibrant and healthy centers of mission
- Leaders who foster change while maintaining orthodoxy and doctrine
- Leaders who delegate the work of the kingdom without abdicating their apostolic role
- Leaders who are intentionally working in passing on the mantle to the next generation of leaders

A survey of the characteristics above and the questions below would assist districts and their leadership teams in assessing their levels of leadership excellence:

- What plans or practices are used to encourage servant leadership in the local church and in the district? Are they intentional and identifiable?
- Is the district encouraging and facilitating mentoring relationships between younger and more seasoned ministers?
- What would mentoring, coaching, or apprenticeship in ministry and leadership on this district look like?

- How do the district mission and strategy inform the pastoral selection process in each congregation?
- How many pastors are able to identify developing ministers and leaders being raised up and trained initially in the local church?

SPIRITUAL VIBRANCY

The prophetic narrative of Ezekiel 37 is relevant for the church today. The church is in a state of disarray, decline, and even death in many areas of the world. There are parts of the world where the church was once vibrant and passionate about God's mission, but today look like the valley of dry bones where the Lord took the prophet. We have often asked ourselves, "Can these bones live?" (v. 3), and we have often answered in despair that "only God knows."

Thus far, we have introduced important strategic and organizational imperatives for districts to effectively fulfill their role as facilitators of church development and missional engagement. These are sound and proven strategies and principles that we have observed work in multiple settings in the world, and we gladly recommend them. However, we are absolutely clear that "unless the LORD builds the house, its builders labor in vain" (Ps. 127:1). Rebuilding the walls of churches and districts that face spiritual anemia cannot be done through systems and organizational practices. Those sound practices must be built on the foundation of the Spirit of God that moves, shapes, and empowers.

As in the biblical narrative of the dry bones, mission, vision, and strategies will be the flesh that will come around dead congregations and provide initial sounds of life. Organizational, educational, and leadership systems and practices will act as the ligaments that will hold these pieces together, but they will not bring life to a district or to a congregation. *Only a passionate pursuit, proclamation, and practice of the powerful presence of God can bring life to our churches and districts!*

The biggest indicator of life and health in a district is the corporate and individual spiritual vibrancy of its leaders and congregations. Spirit-filled leaders follow and join God's movement; they understand that the last, the least, and the lost are not a distraction but our mission; they reach the world on their knees.

The following questions will help district leaders and pastors review some of the areas of spiritual vibrancy in their respective communities and jurisdictions:

- How do you know that God is moving in your district? Is the movement widespread or localized? Give examples or stories.

- What mechanisms or tools are in place to assist pastors and church boards in evaluating the spiritual health of their congregations?
- Do you and your leaders model the life of prayer for your constituents? In what ways?
- How do you measure the effectiveness of the spiritual formation of the district leaders?
- What are the specific means that the district employs to enhance the spiritual vibrancy and well-being of current and future pastors and leaders?

THE FINAL INDICATOR

First and foremost, a healthy district is the aggregate of healthy congregations. These healthy congregations value and maintain the following:

- Harmonious relationships with God, each other, the local community, and the denomination
- Culturally appropriate and harmonious relationships between pastor and key lay leaders
- The global identity and history of the Nazarene family
- Faithfulness to the Great Commission of Christ through active involvement in and with the global mission of the international Church of the Nazarene

- The ability to adapt and change in accordance with the needs of the ministry situation
- Passion for the lost
- Self-sustainability
- Self-propagation and reproduction

A Story

As a regional director of the Eurasia Region, Franklin Cook was intrigued by the history of institutional development of districts in World Mission areas. He was particularly intrigued by the fact that there were districts outside of North America that were far from achieving Phase 3 status, mainly because they did not have the financial resources and economic self-sustainability of their peers in the developed world. However, these districts in developing countries were experiencing incredible movements of God fuelled by an unparalleled missionary zeal. These so-called developing districts seemed to be healthier than most mature districts in the West.

Inspired by these and many other thoughts, the region put together a team of district superintendents and field directors with the purpose of developing a framework and tools for districts in Eurasia. This idea soon germinated and later became the Eurasia Region's District Development Initiative.

Upon Franklin's retirement in 2004, the new regional leadership took on the concept and, in May 2006, a group of district superintendents and leaders from the Eurasia and US/Canada Regions of the Church of the Nazarene gathered in the Netherlands with the purpose of reviewing the assessment tool, restating the purposes of a district, and defining the main health indicators of an effective district.

After several iterations and reviews, the district superintendents in the Eurasia Region gathered in Jordan in April 2007 with the purpose of evaluating and receiving training on the new developmental model. The training focused on the main areas of development and the missional, educational, and organizational dimensions of district health. At the end of the first round of training, district superintendents and field directors (who were later renamed field strategy coordinators) designed assessment and development plans for most of the districts in the region. Four years later, the Eurasia Region can report specific results directly attributable to the implementation of the initiative:

- In 2007 there were four Phase 3 districts in the entire Eurasia Region. All these districts were in Europe, and at least half of them were experiencing missional and/or organizational crises. By the middle of 2011, the Eurasia Region reported ten Phase 3 districts and those original districts with degrees of crises have either developed plans to address the crisis or are already healthy and missional.

- Two-thirds of the districts in the region have their own development plans. Some of these plans include promoting to the next phase, while most of them include specific growth and health plans.

- Thanks to these missional plans, the region grew from approximately 67,000 members and 1,200 organized churches to nearly 210,000 members and 3,300 organized churches in 2011.

- At least half of the districts had missionary district superintendents in 2007. By the middle of 2011, less than one-fourth of the district superintendents in the region are missionaries, while the vast majority are local leaders.

- Thanks to the intentional participation of the district superintendents in the regional Leadership Development Initiative, 90 percent of the districts in the region have identified, trained, and empowered at least twelve new leaders for a total of over four hundred newly developed leaders in a period of four years.

SIX ESSENTIAL CHARACTERISTICS OF A DISTRICT SUPERINTENDENT

5 ⟿ Effective District Superintendents:
The Six Essential Priorities of an Effective Overseer

When district superintendents are elected or appointed to their new assignments, many of them are unaware that they are beginning work for which they have little training. Dr. Robert Clinton, distinguished professor of leadership at Fuller Theological Seminary, describes five types of Christian leaders. Type A leaders are Sunday school teachers, small-group leaders, and committee members. Type B leaders are bivocational pastors and part-time evangelists who minister in smaller churches. Type C leaders are full-time pastors in larger churches that supervise staff members and others. Type D leaders are regional or national leaders over Types A, B, and C leaders. Type E leaders include heads of international organizations.

Concerning Type D leaders (district superintendents), Clinton says:

> Very little effective training is available for Type D leaders. They usually sink or swim on their own. It is this level of leadership that desperately needs mentoring as well as other informal and non-formal training . . . But it is frequently the case that leaders who reach this level see themselves as competent leaders who do not feel the need for further training. They are therefore often blind to the need for training in this critical transition and are too proud to ask for help.[1]

Clinton says that going from Type C leadership to Type D leadership is the most difficult transition for a Christian leader to make. They must cross what he calls the strategic barrier. Type C leaders are involved in doing ministry. They exercise their gifts directly with many people. To be effective, Type D leaders must switch from primarily doing ministry to enabling others to do ministry. They must move from doing direct ministry to indirect ministry; that is, they must cross the strategic barrier. Clinton says Type D leaders must discover that "more time spent with fewer people equals both a greater and a more lasting impact for God."[2] Unfortunately, these leaders have been trained for direct ministry; they do not have training in the leadership skills needed for indirect ministry.

To gain information on this issue and others, ten Nazarene district superintendents gathered to discuss what makes an effective district superintendent. They lead districts that have shown the strongest growth over the last decade (1998-2008). These ten districts started 30 percent of the new church plants in the United States and Canada and gained 20 percent of the new Nazarenes during that decade. Each presented a paper to express his thoughts on how that happened in his district.

As a result of the information shared, some typical assumptions were discovered to be false. Issues such as demographics, organization of the district, personality and talent of the superintendent, and wealth of the district proved of little significance to the growth and progress of the district. We would assume that the districts that had favorable demographics would be the ones growing. However, some of these districts are decreasing.

The demographics of the ten districts varied greatly. One district is mostly urban, found in one of the largest cities in the world populated by many diverse people groups. Another is basically rural with no large metropolitan areas. We assumed that the districts that have talented, charismatic leaders would be growing. But many of these ten leaders are quiet, somewhat shy, and reserved.

Normally, we would believe that the districts that are growing are the ones with great financial reserves and populated by wealthy churches. The reverse is often true. Many of the ten districts were operating on a financial shoestring.

There was no common organizational structure that could be discovered in each district. Some of them divided into mission-focused zones, but most did not. Some of the superintendents had paid assistants, but many did not. So, the question is, were there any similarities or commonalities found in the decadal growth leaders? The answer is, "Most definitely."

1. AN EVANGELISTIC PASSION

Each of the superintendents had a passion to reach lost people *and* were able to communicate this to the district. This was not just an element of their message—winning the lost *was* their message. They looked for ways to tell the stories of lost people finding Jesus and believers finding the joy of the Spirit-filled life. They consistently modeled that evangelism was not just the responsibility of a few but the responsibility of every believer, including the district superintendent.

These superintendents were creative in challenging the district to see their mission field. To keep the focus on people, one superintendent talked about our "1 percent responsibility vision." Nearly eight million people lived in the district and only 42 percent belonged to a church. That means that five million people in the district are unclaimed. They knew they couldn't be responsible for all of them, so they decided to accept responsibility for 1 percent of the unclaimed people on the district. Many pastors have accepted responsibility for 1 percent of the people in their community. The message is creatively repeated often, and the people in the local church understand the 1 percent concept.

Another superintendent, when explaining his mission field, says there are 1.2 million people on the district and 65 percent of them are unchurched. That means 780,000 people on the district need the Lord and good Christian fellowship. Then he explained that most of us know twenty people who are unchurched. That means that if you are in a church averaging fifty in attendance, you are actually in a church of one thousand. There are plenty of people to minister to for Jesus. If we will be moved by the fact that they are lost, have compassion on them, and touch them in the name of Jesus, many will come to Christ. This superintendent constantly speaks in these terms to the people of the district through his preaching and writing.

2. A STRONG EMPHASIS ON CHURCH PLANTING

One of the most productive methods of evangelism is the starting of new churches. Every one of the ten district superintendents placed a high priority on church planting, and he did so without spending large sums of money. One superintendent said, "What we found is that money did not really affect the starting of a congregation nor will money keep them going." Another said, "Planting churches is a part of our consciousness, but certainly not in the same 'norm' as other models across the United States. We have intentionally not poured a lot of finances into starting a church, not that we do not help resource these new works. Our strategy is to be the cheerleader and give permission to those who sense God's movement in the area of planting new communities of believers."

Another superintendent from a metropolitan area, where building costs are prohibitive, said, "We are willing to have church anywhere, anytime, and anyplace . . . We start churches with little or no money at all . . . Several facilities are home to three different language groups on any given Sunday."

These superintendents have been creative in financing church planting. When a property is sold in one district, the proceeds are placed in a segregated account for the purpose of church planting. The superintendent said, "We challenged our pastors and churches to plant a new church and promised if they would, we would return their district budget to them for one year and 50 percent the second year. Of course they had to show that they had invested at least this amount in the new church. The interesting thing that happened was that as we gave money away, God blessed [us] and our reserves did not go down proportionately."

These superintendents understand that the district is not able to plant all the new churches. They continue to encourage churches to plant churches. As one superintendent said, "On our district, we have become comfortable with messy." Not all the church starts survive, and many church planters think and act outside of the norm, but there must be a freedom to experiment and try new ways of reaching people. Presently in the Church of the Nazarene, we are adding churches, but our need is to multiply churches. This will only happen as our pastors discover the joy of church planting. If each pastor will find a nearby city, neighborhood, or people group that is underserved with the gospel and creatively find a way to start a Bible study group there, a new church may develop. Pastors do not need to give away a large group of people to start a church, but perhaps they could train and commission one of their promising leaders to start a church.

One of the districts described their strategy in the following terms:

- Every church is calling every Christian to be engaged in prayer and fasting for a Great Commission movement.
- Every church is intentionally discipling every Christian who is willing.
- Every pastor is raising up and training future pastoral leaders.
- Every church is starting multiple preaching points in the community, working strategically with other mission area churches.
- Every church nurtures at least one preaching point to mission church status each year.

3. A SERIOUS COMMITMENT TO LEADERSHIP DEVELOPMENT

According to professors of missions Gailey and Culbertson, "Leadership development is a key factor in the progress of a cluster of churches on the journey from pioneer to participant."[3] The superintendents in the study often spoke of the importance of loving and supporting all the pastors and leaders on the district. This love and attention was given to the large church and the smaller church without favoritism. Generally, the superintendents did not attend to the large churches only and delegate the smaller churches to someone else's care. Concern was expressed that when the churches were divided in this way, smaller churches would feel they were not important enough for the attention of the district superintendent himself.

A recent study performed by the Nazarene Research Department showed that smaller churches are not a uniform group. Some are certainly in decline, but most small churches are not. Of the small churches that are declining, most are actually larger churches that have become smaller. Churches that have never been larger than one hundred are actually growing faster than the denominational average. Thus, they are making a strong contribution to the overall growth and health of the denomination. Smaller churches really are beautiful and represent an important and viable means of reaching many new people for Jesus with the good news. Small churches need to be celebrated and bivocational pastors made to feel appreciated and loved. The effective superintendent will create a climate of unity by appreciating, celebrating, and tending both the large and the small church.

Most of the ten superintendents interviewed said their work was about accessibility and clear communication. One said, "I believe some of the best ways that have contributed to the district's growth is my accessibility to the pastors as need-ed, weekly newsletters to the pastors, and one-on-one meetings with each pastor on the district. The district superintendent's schedule is printed each week and is available to pastors and laity."

While pastoral care was significant, it was just a part of leadership development. One superinten-dent said, "Our first responsibility in following the movement of God in our area is to invest in people who are being called to become leaders in minis-try. This includes pastors and the laity. No one is exempted from this call. Our second responsibility is to let them lead in the way God directs them to lead. In other words, it may not look like, feel like, be like the way we have always done it, but as God leads us, it will be okay!"

This means giving leaders freedom to work, and then the superintendent becomes the cheerleader. One superintendent said, "Instead of trying to fix blame for mistakes, wise district leaders learn. In-stead of adding rules, they add flexibility. Instead of demanding conformity, they grant permission. Mistakes are a fact of life in a changing world. As one person put it, 'Mistakes are clear evidence that someone out there is trying to do something.'"

Part of leadership development is meeting to-gether and sharing resources. These superinten-dents often have team meetings or staff meetings when the pastors gather for educational and inspirational events. At these meetings one superintendent always has something to distribute. This might include a book, a CD, a DVD, or some sort of handout. By doing so, he is modeling that a good leader is always learning and stretching. There are always new things to learn and new ways of accomplishing the work.

These superintendents have active district training centers. In fact, one district had three schools operating at the same time. These schools are divided by language and location. These superintendents realize that in today's religious climate they will probably have to produce their own leaders. One superintendent said, "Every successful new church plant on our district has been led by a minister already on the district." Louie Bustle often says, "Some of the new churches that will be planted on our districts will be led by pastors who are not even saved yet." They will probably not be able to go to a seminary or university. We must provide training for them and also help them access online training. The modular course of study has become an indispensable tool for our district training centers.

Dr. Eddie Gibbs, professor at Fuller Theological Seminary, makes an interesting observation. In referencing the five spheres of leadership mentioned in Ephesians 4 (pastors, teachers, prophets, evangelists, and apostles), he says that typically seminaries today focus on training the first two—pastors and teachers. He states, "But especially in our post-Christendom, missional context, there is an urgent need to identify the other leadership and ministry functions that Paul identifies, namely the apostle, prophet, and evangelist." Could it be that our district training centers can effectively train, encourage, and validate those called to pioneer churches and speak prophetically? We are not suggesting that our formal educational institutions are not effective in their work. They are, but today's realities suggest that many called persons are unable to move away and enter a school. It is incumbent upon the district to provide effective local training centers to train leaders so that many new churches can be planted. Gibbs quotes Martin Garner, who said, "Apostolic leadership provides an essential element for the new emerging church . . . This issue of the development of a new kind of leadership is possibly the single most important question of strategy in this decade, and whether the church responds correctly or not will determine to some extent its survival as a viable expression of the gospel in the years to come."

4. AN AWARENESS OF THE
ART OF PASTORAL PLACEMENT

Effective superintendents understand that pastoral placement is more than just filling pulpits. However, if the superintendent is intentional in finding the right pastor for the right church, the work will flourish. These ten superintendents were committed to finding passionate, missional, soul-winning pastors for their districts. One superintendent talked about his approach at the pastor's installation service. He always says something like this to the pastor: "I am not asking you to just fill this pulpit. I am asking you to embrace this community, this city." The pastor's task is not just to preach. He must see himself as responsible for the mission of God in this city.

One superintendent said in regard to finding pastors, "I adopted a policy that has served me well. Ask the best and let them tell you no." This has enabled him to secure many fine pastors to his district. Several of the superintendents followed this adage: The best predictor of future behavior is past behavior. They gave more credence to the minister's profile in the General Secretary's Office than to the candidate's resume. If the profile indicates that the minister had relatively long tenures, received new members by profession of faith, and was faithful in leading the church to pay budgets in the past, this is a strong indication that the superintendent will do the same in the future. When the superintendent is prayerful and careful in the selection of his pastors, he or she will be rewarded with a fine team of pastors who embrace the kingdom of Christ and see it move forward.

5. THE ABILITY TO CROSS THE STRATEGIC BARRIER

Earlier, Dr. Robert Clinton is quoted as saying that Type D leaders must learn how to change from direct to indirect ministry. To be effective as district superintendents, they must cross the strategic barrier. They must learn how to minister through other leaders. Without an overall strategy, all of their time will be spent handling urgent details and refereeing church conflicts. The superintendent has been placed in this role to give direction and shape a desired future, and the starting point is studying the culture of the district. Some of the ten superintendents arrived at a strategy intuitively, and others went through a more formal process.

One superintendent described how he began his task: "As I began to pray, talk, and listen to pastors, and drive through the cities and towns of my district, the picture began to emerge . . . the key to our future is healthy pastors, healthy churches, and new congregations. So this has been our primary focus for the last eight years." He decided to find an assistant who would work with administration, finances, property issues, and the pastors' education program. This would free the superintendent to stamp his leaders with his philosophy. He often spoke of having courage and taking risks, and encouraged his pastors by saying, "Just go ahead." He discovered that 45 percent of the district was Hispanic, so he focused much of his attention on finding and developing leaders who are now successfully planting Hispanic churches all over the district. In other words, he studied his district and developed a strategy. His work went beyond just loving and caring for the pastors on the district. Pastoral care done by the superintendent is important work, but it is not all of his work. Superintendents must learn how to influence through other leaders.

One superintendent serves a district that is so large and diverse that it has approximately 10 percent of the United States' population living within the district borders. This could be overwhelming, but he now thinks of his district as a foreign mission field. The leaders of his district must think and live cross-culturally every day. This district superintendent's strategy took shape as the superintendent became a student of the district. He learned that 75 percent of the pastoral families are bivocational and that 51 percent of the churches do not own buildings. Only after learning these and similar facts could he gather other leaders around the mission field.

One of the ten superintendents was born and raised on his district. He left for just a few years to attend school, but came back to pastor there. Later he was elected district superintendent and has served there for many years. Because he has lived and worked there so long, he is aware of the culture. He understands it. He knows how to navigate it. He makes sure the pastors come to understand it. Each district is unique and the strategies emerge as the superintendent and his leaders ask the question, Who has God placed in our mission field and what is our strategy to reach them with the gospel?

6. A HEALTHY BALANCE BETWEEN GROWTH AND GODLINESS

Effective superintendents are at home leading both a prayer retreat and a board retreat. They are both growth-oriented and heavenly-minded. They look outward and upward. They are persons of prayer. One superintendent kept a photo of each of the pastors and spouses in his district on the wall of his prayer room. Those photos helped him call out their names in prayer. One superintendent said, "We must work hard, preach the Word, major on outreach, dream, think, hope, and make no little plans. Remember that you must go to your knees daily in prayer—pray in the services, pray with the people, pray alone, pray at home, pray as you drive, pray everywhere."

In speaking of spiritual leadership, one of the superintendents said, "A district superintendent must authentically live out each day in close relationship with God and with those he serves. Someone recently said to me, 'Nothing happens without prayer and everything that happens without prayer is nothing.' I can't imagine trying to lead a district without an intimate prayer life. I have found that God transforms people and situations far beyond my capacities to change them when I bring them to God in prayer. I am convinced prayer is the essential, indispensable foundation for leading any endeavor, especially a district in need of revitalization. District superintendents must pray about everything."

A district superintendent in the Church of the Nazarene must exhibit sanctified integrity. To gain the support of the pastors and churches on the district, he or she must treat everyone with honesty and respect. They will know immediately if the superintendent's preaching does not match his or her life, and if they sense a discrepancy, they will begin to ignore the superintendent's leadership.

Conversely, people will respond to superintendents who lead and preach with sanctified passion.

Ultimately, the work of the superintendent is spiritual work. If the church is to grow, God will be the one to transform lives. If sinners are saved, God will do it. If believers are sanctified wholly, God will be the one to accomplish it. The effective superintendent challenges churches and pastors to grow, depends on God to bring the increase, and waters the whole process with prayer.

Conclusion
It Can Be Done

Perhaps the district superintendent who is reading this now feels overwhelmed, unprepared, and personally ill-equipped for the work before him or her. You say, "I am not a ten-talented person. I am not a skilled orator, an organizational genius, or a gifted strategist. I am afraid I am not prepared or even capable of such work." If you feel that way, listen to this good news.

We have intentionally not mentioned the names of the ten superintendents or the districts they serve. These leaders want no credit for their work. God receives the glory. However, there are two names that must be mentioned. For eighteen years, Charles and Mary Thompson served as the district superintendents of the Virginia District. One Sunday night, the Thompsons visited the Harrisburg Church. After preaching, Charles prayed this closing prayer: "Lord, whatever it takes, please drive the Virginia District to her knees in prayer." On the way home that night, the Thompsons were involved in a horrific car accident with an eighteen-wheeler. It took a long time to free Charles and

Mary from the wreckage. Thinking Charles was dead, the paramedics placed him in a body bag. The district was driven to her knees, and, miraculously, Charles survived.

For a number of months, the district gathered around the recuperating Thompson and the pastors did the work of the district superintendent. When Charles came back to work, he was not the same man. His speech was a bit slurred. He sometimes forgot names. He was greatly weakened. He was no longer strong in administration. He was no longer an impressive figure. But something beautiful began to happen. Even though his pastors knew his weaknesses and shortcomings, they still worked hard because they couldn't bear to think of letting Charles down. They couldn't stand the thought of Charles being disappointed. There was no way that the pastors would vote against him at recall time. They loved him too much. He was disabled, but they honored him.

Charles Thompson lost much as a result of the accident, but he still had two important things.

He was a man of prayer. Two or three times a year, he would call the pastors to a prayer summit. He wouldn't lead these prayer times, but he was there. He always stayed in the back of the room. A Virginia pastor reported that on one occasion, he had to leave the prayer time early. They were meeting in a hotel ballroom. The lights were dimmed. As this pastor made his way to the back of the room, there in the darkness, he stumbled over Charles. He was lying on his face by the back door. The district superintendent was praying and calling out the names of his pastors, asking God to bless their ministries. The pastor was moved.

There was one other thing Charles had. He was a man of passion. He couldn't get through his report at district assembly without weeping. One of his pastors reported that generally when he would come for his annual visit, he wouldn't want to preach. He would just say, "Well, Mary and I want to come to church just to support you and pray for you. We will just slip in." But one Sunday, the pastor prevailed on Charles to preach. The pastor had noticed that the church was going through a dry spell and people were not using the altar freely during the altar calls. Charles preached that morning. The pastor said the sermon wasn't all that good, maybe a four out of ten. Charles just wept his way through it. Then he opened the altar, and the altar flooded with seekers.

A few years ago when he retired, he immediately prevailed upon the new district superintendent to let him have a church. He needed to keep preaching; he needed for God to use him. The most important thing to Charles Thompson was to pray and reach people. With a smile, he accepted a little church of thirty people, and it quickly grew to one hundred.

This disabled, halting-tongued, shy, humble superintendent and his faithful wife led uncommonly well. And ironically, the Virginia District had the strongest decadal growth rates of all the districts in the United States and Canada. Charles Thompson knew how to recognize good pastors. He knew how to encourage them along the way. He knew how to release them and trust them. But most of all, he knew how to pray and weep. Could there be a secret here? Could it be so obvious we have missed it? He was not an administrator. He was a man of God. He was not a manager. He was a man of passion. And the pastors and laypersons of the Virginia District knew it. They loved him. They gathered around him. They shared the load so that many people were added to the kingdom.

And if Charles Thompson could lead a growing district, you can too.

Appendix

DISTRICT DEVELOPMENT SELF-STUDY SURVEY

Note to Leadership: This self-study is designed to help districts help churches fulfill their mission. The areas of self-study are not limited to the questions below, but they could assist districts and their leadership teams in assessing their current capacity to fulfill their purpose. The questions are open-ended, leaving room for discussion, analysis, and synthesis.

1. BACKGROUND INFORMATION

   a. How long has the Church of the Nazarene been in existence in the district area?

   b. What has been the history of leadership in the district (district superintendents, tenure, etc.)?

   c. What is the history of growth and/or decline in the district?

   d. How has the district partnered with local churches in church planting?

   e. How many churches have been started and/or incubated in the district, which developed into organized churches?

   f. How many churches have been started that did not mature? Why?

2. MISSIONAL DEFINITION

   a. What is the spoken and unspoken mission of the district (written and unwritten) in fifteen words or less? How is it communicated? How often?

b. Can we trace the direct influence of the district mission on local church missional activities where the mission is being lived out? Give examples or stories.

c. Do churches in the district recognize their missional role as inspired by the mission statement? How do you know?

d. To what degree is there a clear and compelling vision at work on our district that inspires passion and gives direction to our congregations?

e. Do churches in the district have specific evangelism, church planting, discipleship, and community engagement plans that are reflective of their missional commitment?

3. ORGANIZATIONAL EFFECTIVENESS

a. How is the district organized for mission implementation?

b. To what degree do district boards, committees, and organizations reflect the mission priority of the district? How do you measure their missional effectiveness and integration?

c. What are the mechanisms that the district uses to receive feedback on the fulfillment of its missional priorities? Are there other teams or groups that help the district accomplish and review its missional priorities (e.g., mission strategy, re-visioning board, etc.)?

   d. What are the platforms that the district uses to allow new missional ideas to take place within the ministry of the church in the district?

   e. What activities of the district superintendent and staff are on target missionally? What activities of the district superintendent and staff tend to move them off mission?

   f. Is the district budget reflective of the missional priorities of the district? What portion of your funds should be spent directly on missional activities? What percentage actually is spent for this purpose rather than overhead?

4. DOCTRINAL INTEGRITY

   a. What methods, practices, and means does the district employ to maintain and promote doctrinal integrity before the churches?

   b. What is the strategy that the district employs to articulate and promote the core beliefs and values (Christian, holiness, missional) of the Church of the Nazarene?

   c. To what degree are lay leaders in our congregations familiarized with and committed to the Agreed Statement of Belief? Articles of Faith? Core Values?

   d. What are some ways that the district superintendent engages pastors in theological reflection and development of a pastoral theology consistent with our Nazarene identity?

e. How does the district ensure that new church plants are grounded on the core doctrine of the Church of the Nazarene?

5. EDUCATIONAL PRIORITY

a. What is the district strategy to recruit, mentor, and train leaders for ministry service? Include comments about education toward ordination, curriculum, reading materials, and district-sponsored workshops or seminars.

b. What mechanisms does the district have to help its pastors understand, share, and adequately articulate the central doctrines of the Church of the Nazarene?

c. What is the district strategy for providing continuing education and training for ministers?

d. How do you describe the relationship of the district to its theological education institutions?

e. What are the tracks available for preparation for ordination? Do they include the major language groups of the district?

f. Are there specific educational initiatives in the district designed to prepare ministers and laypersons for evangelism, church planting, and community outreach?

6. LEADERSHIP EXCELLENCE

a. What plans or practices are used to encourage and strengthen leadership in the local church and in the district? Are they intentional and identifiable?

b. Is the district encouraging and facilitating mentoring relationships between younger and more seasoned ministers?

c. Provide a picture of what mentoring, coaching, or apprenticeship in ministry and leadership on this district would look like.

d. How do the district mission and strategy inform the pastoral selection process in each congregation?

e. How many pastors are able to identify developing ministers and leaders being raised up and trained initially in the local church?

f. Are there district events that are designed for testing a call into vocational ministry?

7. SPIRITUAL VIBRANCY

a. How do you know that God is moving on your district? Is the movement widespread or localized? Give examples or stories.

b. What mechanisms/tools are in place to assist pastors and church boards in evaluating the spiritual health of their congregations?

c. Do you and your leaders model the life of prayer for your constituents? In what ways?

d. How do you measure the effectiveness of the spiritual formation of the district leaders?

e. What are the specific means that the district employs to enhance the spiritual vibrancy and well-being of current and future pastors and leaders?

REVIEW PROCESS:
CONCLUSIONS AND PLANS

This self-assessment tool has been designed to help districts and their leaders get a comprehensive picture of the district's health. There are at least five key areas that the district could identify as areas to target. Prayerfully consider and list them:

1. _____

   _____

2. _____

   _____

3. _____

   _____

4. _____

   _____

5. _____

   _____

This may be a good time to prayerfully consider a district development plan designed to respond to those areas that hinder the district's effectiveness in helping churches fulfill their mission to make Christlike disciples in the nations.

Notes

Chapter 1

1. Church of the Nazarene, "Mission," Board of General Superintendents, http://www.nazarene.org/ministries/superintendents/mission/display.aspx (accessed August 3, 2011).

Chapter 2

1. Craig Keener, *The IVP Bible Background Commentary: New Testament* (Downers Grove, Ill.: InterVarsity Press, 1993).

2. Hugo Alvarado, "Pasado, Herencia, y Gesta Autoctona—Una Resena Historica de la Iglesia del Nazareno en Guatemala," Didache: Faithful Teaching. http://didache.nazarene.org/index.php?searchword=hugo&ordering=&searchphrase=all&Itemid=29&option=com_search (accessed August 8, 2011).

3. David Garrison, *Church Planting Movements: How God Is Redeeming a Lost World* (Midlothian, Va.: WIGTake Resources, 2004).

4. *100 Years of Mission* (Kansas City: Nazarene Publishing House, 2008), 27-32.

5. Charles Gailey and Howard Culbertson, *Discovering Missions* (Kansas City: Beacon Hill Press of Kansas City, 2007), 208.

6. Contributed by Debra Hamrick from the Los Angeles District. Debra led a district-wide work team to Sri Lanka.

7. 2007 Mid-Atlantic District Assembly Journal.

Chapter 3

1. *Church of the Nazarene Manual 2009-2013* (Kansas City: Nazarene Publishing House, 2009), 106.

Chapter 4

1. Ibid.

2. Paul Borden, *Hit the Bullseye: How Denominations Can Aim the Congregation at the Mission Field* (Nashville: Abingdon Press, 2003).

3. Bryan Barry, *Strategic Planning Workbook for Non-Profit Organizations* (Minneapolis: Fieldstone Alliance, 2006), 6.

4. Borden, *Hit the Bullseye*, 45-47.

5. Jerry Porter, "Taking Responsibility for Results: Growth Never Comes by Settling for the Status Quo," *Holiness Today* 13, no. 3 (2011).

6. Gustavo Crocker, *Developing a Missional Church "The Jesus Way"* (2011), 47.

7. These and subsequent questions are included in the appendix as the District Development Self-Assessment Survey that districts could use to stimulate thinking, planning, and missional engagement.

8. Louis Sullivan, "The Tall Office Building Artistically Considered," *Lippincott's Magazine* (March 1896).

9. Thomas Peters and Robert Waterman Jr., *In Search of Excellence: Lessons from America's Best-Run Companies* (New York: Harper & Row Publishers, 1982).

10. Gustavo Crocker, "Total Quality of Charitable Service: Profiles of Excellence in Christian Relief and Development Organizations" (PhD diss., Regent University, 2001).

11. A. W. Tozer, *Man, the Dwelling Place of God* (Camp Hill, Pa.: Christian Publications, 1966).

12. *Church of the Nazarene Manual 2009-2013*, 181.

13. Ibid.

14. Borden, *Hit the Bullseye*, 56.

Chapter 5

1. Robert Clinton, *The Making of a Leader* (Colorado Springs, Colo.: NavPress 1988).

2. Ibid.

3. Gailey and Culbertson, *Discovering Missions*, 59.